CELINE DION
TAKING CHANCES

Management: **Rene Angelil**
FEELING PRODUCTIONS INC.
In Montreal:
2540 Daniel-Johnson Blvd., #755
Laval, Quebec, Canada H7T 2S3

Executive Assistant to Celine Dion and
 Rene Angelil: **Sylvie Beauregard**
Executive Vice-President Finance and
 Administration: **Gilles Lapointe**

In Toronto:
4141 Yonge St, Suite 305
Toronto, Ontario, Canada M2P 2A8

Management Associate: **Dave Platel**
Director, Marketing
 Operations: **Lina Attisano**

Alfred Publishing gives a special thanks to Dave Platel for his
loyalty to us since the passing of our dear friend Ben Kaye.

TEAM *Celine* DION

Official Online Fan Club at www.**celine**dion.com

Alfred Publishing Co., Inc.
16320 Roscoe Blvd., Suite 100
P.O. Box 10003
Van Nuys, CA 91410-0003
alfred.com

ISBN-10: 1-7390-5105-9
ISBN-13: 978-1-7390-5105-4

CONTENTS

TAKING CHANCES

Words and Music by
KARA DIOGUARDI and
DAVID STEWART

Moderately slow ♩ = 92

Verse 1:

1. Don't know much a - bout your life.

Don't know much a - bout your world,____ but____ don't

wan - na be a - lone to - night____ on____ this plan - et they____ call Earth..

Taking Chances - 7 - 1
29219

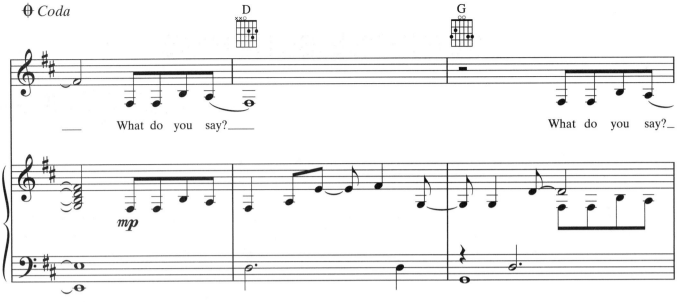

SURPRISE SURPRISE

Words and Music by
KARA DIOGUARDI, MARTIN HARRINGTON
and ASH HOWES

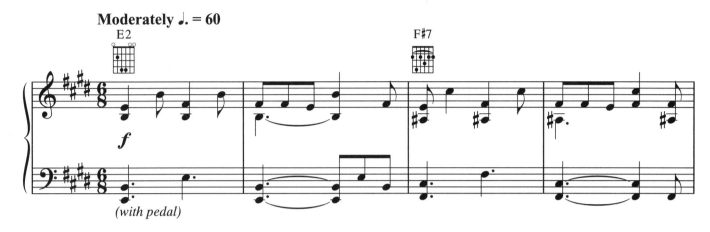

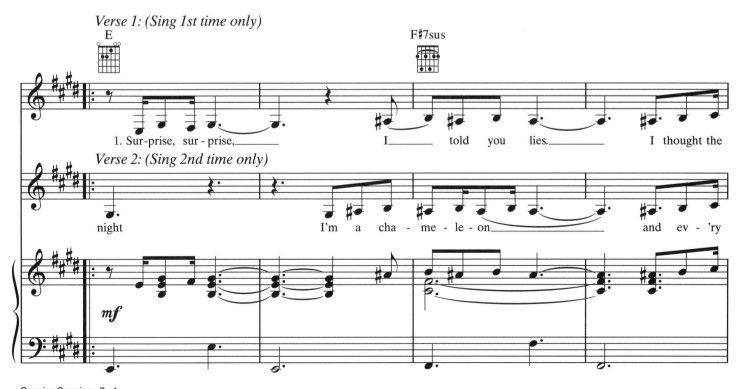

Surprise Surprise - 7 - 1
29219

16

Bridge:

And it's in your eyes,_____ that it's all or noth-ing.__

What I can't dis-guise is that you're on to some-thing. I

let my-self go, will you still want me? Will I be e-nough? The fear of that haunts me.__

'Cause what if you_ walk a - way?_____ Just when you

18 *Chorus:*

ALONE

Words and Music by
BILLY STEINBERG and THOMAS KELLY

1. I hear the tick-ing of the clock, I'm ly-ing here, the
2. You don't know how long I have want-ed to touch your lips and

room's pitch dark.
hold you tight,

oh.

I won-der where you are to-night,
You don't know how long I have

wait-ed, and I was gon-na

no an-swer on the tel-e-phone.
tell you to-night.

EYES ON ME

Words and Music by
KRISTIAN LUNDIN, SAVAN KOTECHA
and DELTA GOODREM

Verse:

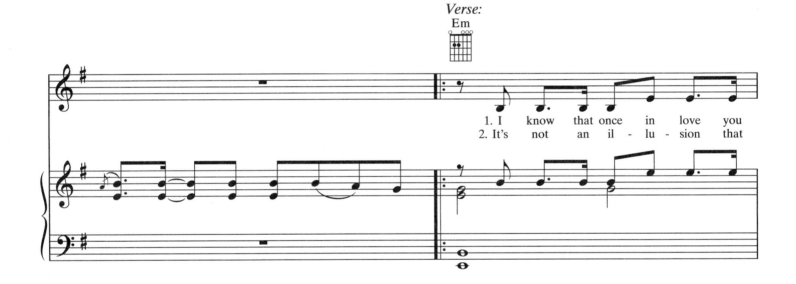

1. I know that once in love you
2. It's not an il - lu - sion that

don't_ think of the dev - il who's in - side._
you're_ the one and I have fal - len deep._

Eyes on Me - 8 - 1
29219

Chorus:

mine,_____ so you bet-ter say yeah,_____ No mat-ter what you think I need,_ no, it

does-n't real-ly mat-ter what you once be-lieved._ say yeah. I wan-na be the air you breathe._Yeah, you

So you bet-ter say yeah. bet-ter be ev-'ry-thing you said you'd be.____ I bet-ter be the on-ly one__ or

we can't_ go on, no mat-ter what you think I need._____ You bet-ter

28

Eyes on Me - 8 - 5
29219

MY LOVE

Words and Music by
LINDA PERRY

did you know___ that I would play___ the part?___

I must have made it clear right from___ the start. start.

Bridge:

I would share___ my whole___ life___ with you.___

Would you do___ the same___ for me?___

SHADOW OF LOVE

Words and Music by
ANDERS BAGGE, ALDO NOVA
and PETER SJOSTROM

Moderately ♩ = 116

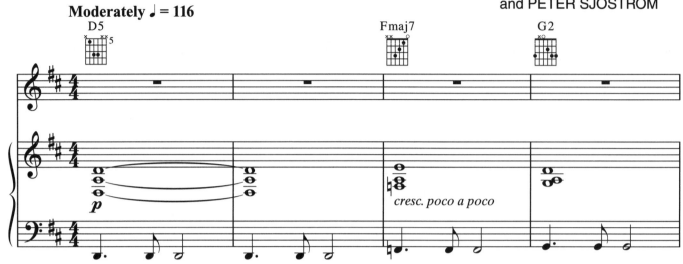

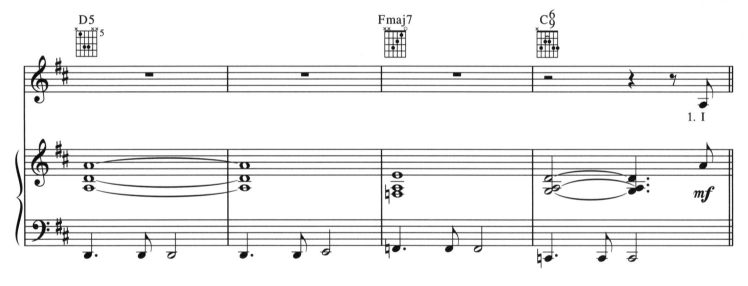

Verse:

live my life___ like a run-a-way. I hide my dreams___ in a
love sur-rounds__ me, it's ev-er-y-where.__ It is my shel-ter, it

42

love,_____ love, love, yeah. To me you are_ the on - ly one_

_____ I_ dream_____ of,_____

Repeat ad lib. and fade

____ 'cause I'm liv - in' in the shad-ow of love._____

THIS TIME

Words and Music by
BEN MOODY, DAVID HODGES
and STEVEN McMORRAN

NEW DAWN

Words and Music by
LINDA PERRY

Slowly ♩ = 69

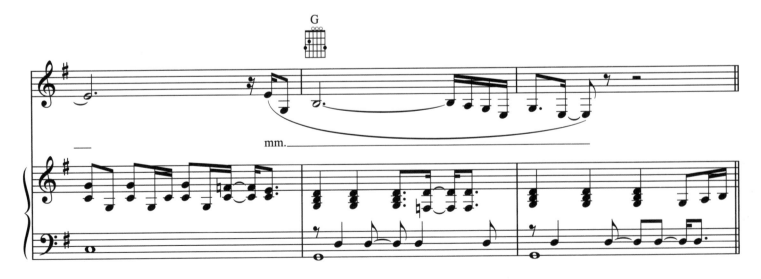

New Dawn - 6 - 1
29219

52

54

A SONG FOR YOU

Words and Music by
ANDERS BAGGE, ALDO NOVA
and ROBERT WELLS

Slowly and freely ♩ = 69

58

Then I hope you'll un-der-stand_____

once you've lis-tened till the end.

Heard the mu-sic in my head, so be-

A WORLD TO BELIEVE IN

Words by
ROSANNA CICIOLA

Music by
TINO IZZO

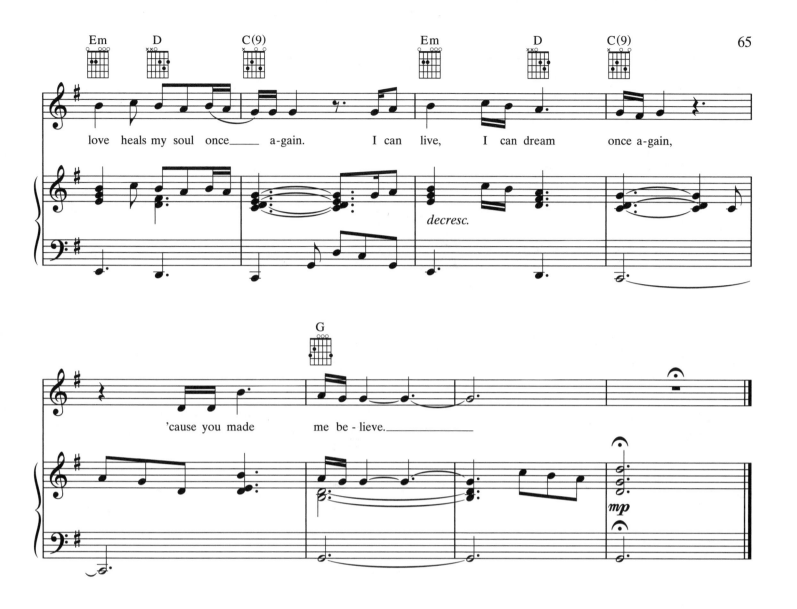

Verse 2:
I know that dreams we hold on to can just fade away.
And I know that words can be wasted with so much to say.
And I when I feel helpless, there's always a hope that shines through
And makes me believe, makes me believe.
And I see for one fleeting moment
A paradise under the sun.
I drift away and I make my way back to you.
You gave me faith.
(To Chorus:)

CAN'T FIGHT THE FEELIN'

Moderately slow rock ♩ = 84

Words and Music by
ALDO NOVA

I GOT NOTHIN' LEFT

Words and Music by
SHAFFER SMITH and CHARLES HARMON

RIGHT NEXT TO THE RIGHT ONE

Words and Music by
TIM CHRISTENSEN

Right Next to the Right One - 6 - 2
29219

80

Bridge:

Chorus:

FADE AWAY

Words and Music by
PEER ASTROM, DAVID STENMARCK
and ALDO NOVA

88

Coda

Bm ... A ...

that bring____ you____ down.____ You know____ that

Chorus:

Bm ... G ... D ...

once____ touched____ by____ pain,____ you're not_____ the same.___

A/C# ... Bm ... G ...

___ But____ time____ can____ heal____ your heart____

Bm ... A/C# ... G ...

___ a - gain.____ So____ let____ the____ clouds_____

THAT'S JUST THE WOMAN IN ME

Words and Music by
KIMBLERLY REW

94

That's Just the Woman in Me - 7 - 5
29219

SKIES OF L.A.

Words and Music by
TERIUS NASH, CHRISTOPHER STEWART
and THADDIS HARRELL

Slowly, with a longing feel ♩ = 69

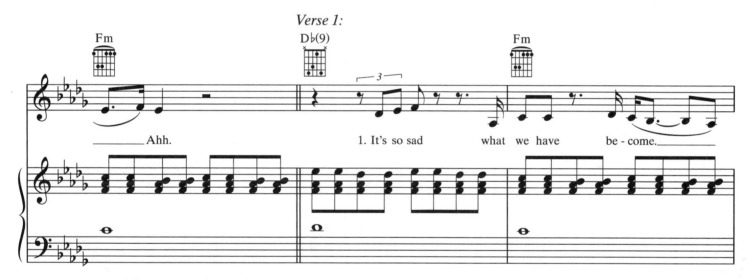

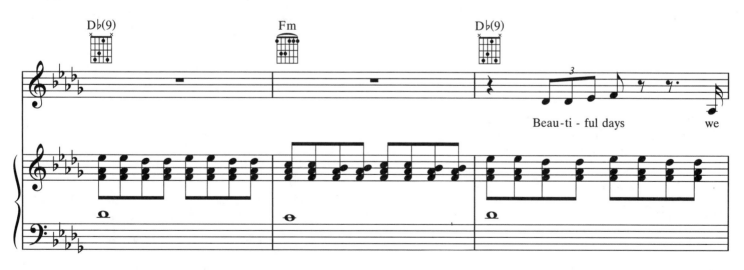

Skies of L.A. - 7 - 1
29219